SWIMMER

By SHELLEY GILL

Illustrated by SHANNON CARTWRIGHT

Lisa

To Adventure!!

Shelley Gill
1996

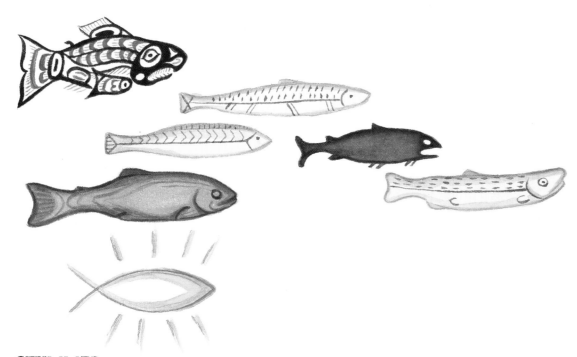

SWIMMER

Text copyright 1995 Shelley Gill
Illustrations copyright 1995 Shannon Cartwright

Paws IV Publishing
P.O. Box 2364
Homer, Alaska 99603

Library of Congress Number: 93-086371
The story of the Chinook salmon -
Swimmer's journey over 10,000 miles
illustrates the cycles of life for the
salmon and the girl Katya who is
coming of age. 32 pages full color.
ISBN 0-93400723-3 cloth
ISBN 0-934007-24-1 paper
Printed in the USA on recycled paper
First edition April 1995
987654321

For Nani - whose spirit rests in the deep blue waters of the Gulfstream
S.G.
For Paul and Dorothy - who introduced me to the magic of the salmon
S.C.

Special thanks to biologists Bill Bushur, Henry Yuen,
Suzi Lozo and Richard Barnes and Bethel elder Elena Charles and all the kids and parents from Newtok,
Atmautlauk, Napaskiak and Kwethluk who helped me understand yaaruiq

The Yukon River is the 5th largest river in North America. For the 10-15,000 Native Alaskans who live along its shores salmon are very important-each species is used for food. Salmon are eaten fresh, smoked, dried, salted and canned. Dried King salmon skins have also been used for mukluk bottoms and as decorations on parkas.

In the fading glow of the midnight sun, Katya watched the net, waiting for the telltale jerking motion. This was her sixth year at fish camp and just as she knew leaves fell from the trees each autumn, she knew the salmon would soon return from the sea.

She knew because her grandmother told her stories of the great Chinook, king of all salmon. She knew because she remembered the prayer her grandmother had taught her:

"Oh swimmers, thank you for coming to us," Katya whispered, cutting the long shape of the salmon in the sand with an ivory knife. "Swimmer we honor you."

It was an ancient prayer of thanks to the fish that had fed her people for thousands of years.

Most Native people who live along the Yukon and its tributaries have traditional lifestyles. Yupik Eskimo villages are located along the coast and the lower 300 miles of the river. Athabascan Indians are found along the upper river and throughout Interior Alaska. For centuries Native people have moved to fish camps each spring to await the salmon.

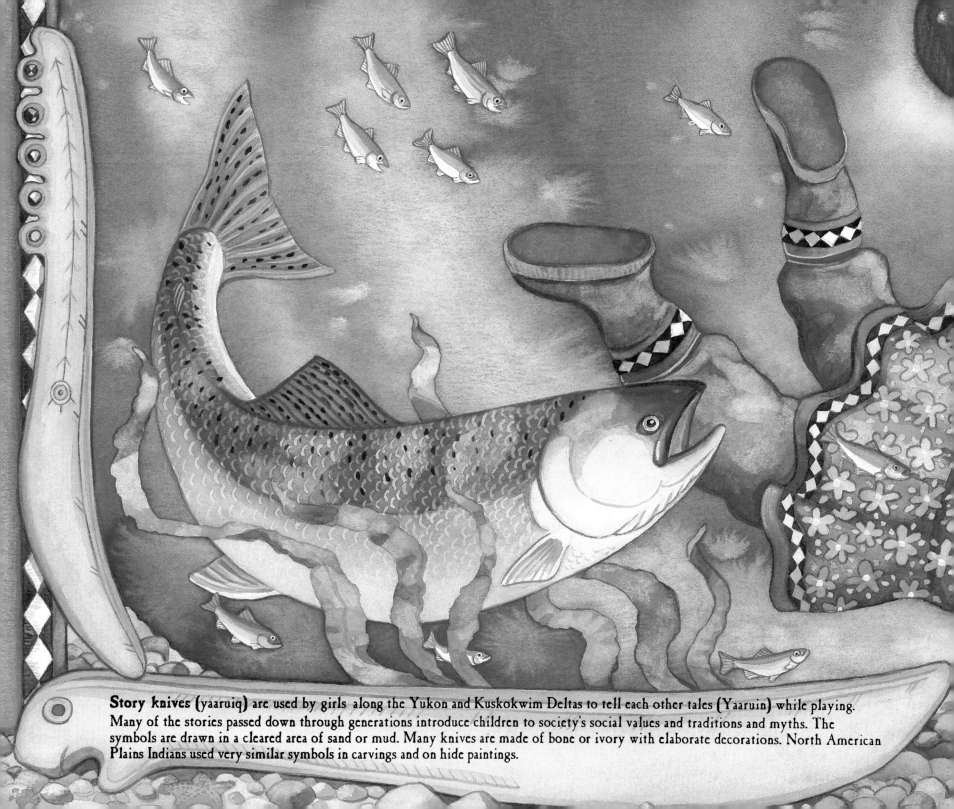

Story knives (yaaruiq) are used by girls along the Yukon and Kuskokwim Deltas to tell each other tales (Yaaruin) while playing. Many of the stories passed down through generations introduce children to society's social values and traditions and myths. The symbols are drawn in a cleared area of sand or mud. Many knives are made of bone or ivory with elaborate decorations. North American Plains Indians used very similar symbols in carvings and on hide paintings.

Katya imagined she was a sleek salmon gliding through the icy waters of the Bering Sea. Swimming in deep places, surrounded by shadow creatures, rising to dance beneath the northern lights.

But time is a circle, the girl knew. One day a gleaming silver, the Chinook soon grows old, their skin turning red, the splash from their leaping a fitful death song. When they returned from the sea only one task remained.

They must lay their eggs in the river.
It all happened in the river.
Birth and death.
Beginning and end.

In the beginning the bright red leaves from the blueberry bushes spilled across the tundra. Above the treeline the ground was bright with snow. At dawn a skim of ice clung to the rocks that dotted Caribou Creek. Just beneath the twisted limb of an old birch, deep in the river gravel, lay thousands of orange eggs---an underwater nursery.

As the days grew shorter and colder, the world around the nest grew white and silent. Winter deepened and the eggs began to change color, first to deep orange then pale apricot.

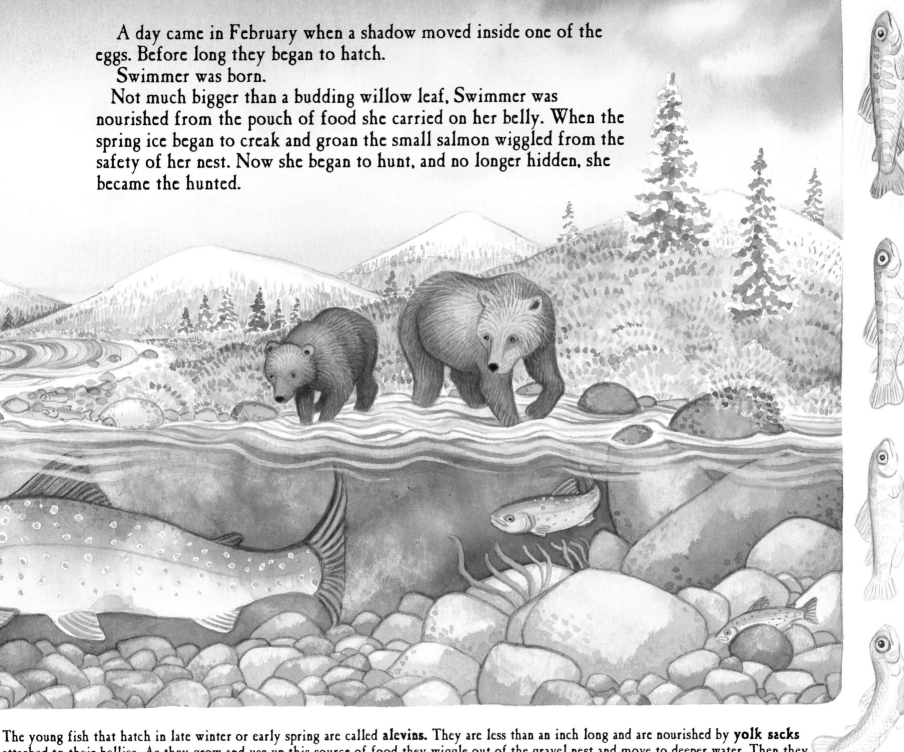

A day came in February when a shadow moved inside one of the eggs. Before long they began to hatch.

Swimmer was born.

Not much bigger than a budding willow leaf, Swimmer was nourished from the pouch of food she carried on her belly. When the spring ice began to creak and groan the small salmon wiggled from the safety of her nest. Now she began to hunt, and no longer hidden, she became the hunted.

The young fish that hatch in late winter or early spring are called **alevins.** They are less than an inch long and are nourished by **yolk sacks** attached to their bellies. As they grow and use up this source of food they wiggle out of the gravel nest and move to deeper water. Then they are referred to as **fry.**

Above the frozen ice, otters scampered and moose foraged. Beneath the ice, Swimmer fought for her life.

Grayling darted through the shallows, feasting on baby salmon. As the ice melted, predators from the sky joined the hunt. Swimmer hid in the river's dark bends and as the days grew longer she sank deeper into a shadow world, eating insect larvae, hiding in the rocks.

These baby salmon swim in groups and feed on tiny plants and animals. They are called fingerlings or **parr** and have dark spots on their sides known as **parr marks**. These help the parr stay camouflaged in the river rocks. At this stage of life a variety of fish and birds are the salmon's greatest enemies.

As the brown spring gave way to summer green, Swimmer grew. She would spend two years in fresh water before leaving on a great journey to the salty water of the sea. Her skin grew silver scales as she began her move to deep water, hunting by night, hiding by day. She was surrounded by thousands of other salmon, all of them feeding, many of them becoming food. Swimmer was lucky. She survived, drifting down the creek until she reached the big water, the great muddy Yukon, her highway to the sea.

As the parr leave fresh water and migrate to the sea they undergo a process called **smolting**. Their body must adapt to the salt water, otherwise the salt would dehydrate them. Scientists think this change in body chemistry is triggered by sunlight and temperature.

Salmon are very nearsighted, but they see movement and contrast. They have great senses of smell, hearing and taste that help them find food and sense danger. They also feel sound and pressure waves against the length of their body.

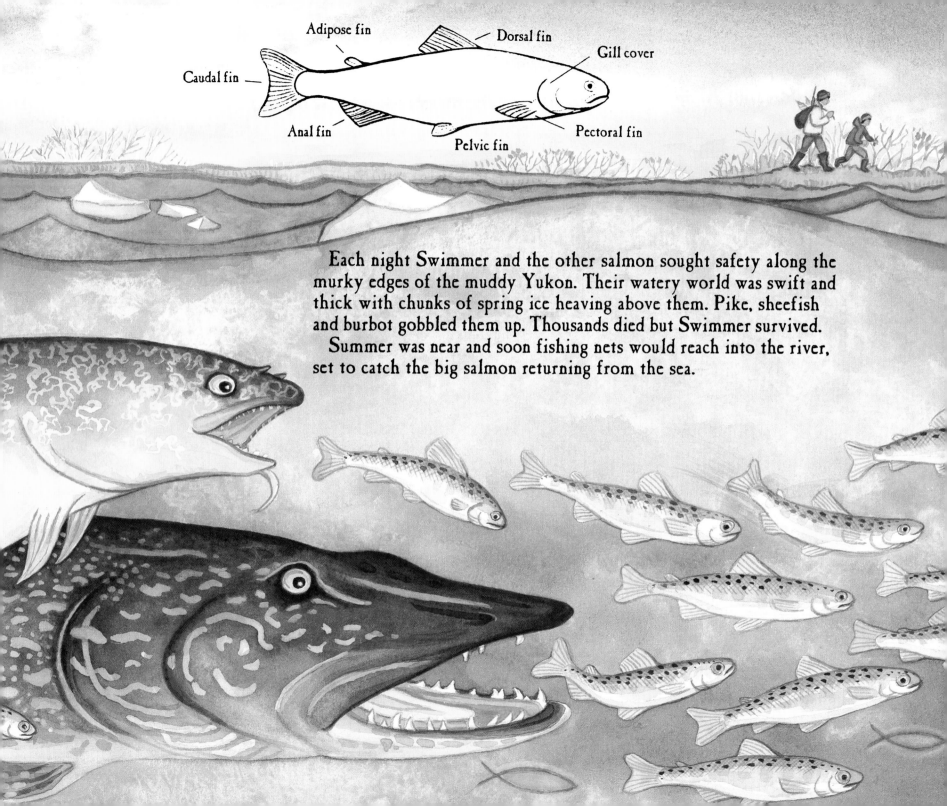

Adipose fin

Dorsal fin

Gill cover

Caudal fin

Anal fin

Pelvic fin

Pectoral fin

Each night Swimmer and the other salmon sought safety along the murky edges of the muddy Yukon. Their watery world was swift and thick with chunks of spring ice heaving above them. Pike, sheefish and burbot gobbled them up. Thousands died but Swimmer survived.

Summer was near and soon fishing nets would reach into the river, set to catch the big salmon returning from the sea.

Beyond the wide river was the Delta and here Swimmer lingered. She sensed a change in the motion of the water, a first taste of salt in the tide. She fed on rich clouds of tiny marine creatures and shrimp that floated in the shallow waters. She grew bigger and stronger, and then one day she was there, in the boundless sea that had called to her since birth.

Like the **growth rings** of a tree, the scales of the salmon also show annual growth rings. Some growth sections are wider than others, probably because the salmon sometimes live an easier life and grow faster than during tough times. As the salmon enter fresh water, their scales begin to be absorbed into the body. They are readable however and yield valuable age and genetic information used by biologists to pinpoint the spawning stream of origin.

The Yukon and Kuskokwim Rivers deposit enough silt to form one of the world's major coastal flood plains, the 200 mile long and 250 mile wide Yukon-Kuskokwim Delta. About half of the delta is wet, covered with ponds, lakes, rivers, streams and tidal flats. The rest is treeless tundra. Warm ocean currents provide a constant source of plankton that arrives with each ocean tide. This fertile area supports 170 species of birds, some of which migrate from as far away as the Antarctic.

Plankton

The northern Pacific Ocean is home to five species of salmon. The Humpy or Pink weighs an average 4 lbs.; the Chum or Dog salmon weighs about 9 lbs. and gets his name because he is the favorite fish to power dogteams in the Arctic; the Silver or Coho weighs about 9 lbs.; the Sockeye or Red about 6 lbs. and the Chinook or King weighs an average 22 lbs. and is about 36 inches long. A big King can weigh up to 100 lbs. All five species of salmon are bright silver while living in the ocean. Here they are pictured in spawning colors.

Cruising at sea speed, leaping through the dark wall of waves, Swimmer pushed further into the blue black distance, away from the scent of her home river. She stored knowledge of currents and eddies in each nerve that passed from her gills to her tail. As the sea moved through the earth's magnetic field, tiny electrical surges helped her navigate.

From a hundred creeks, through a dozen rivers, thousands of other salmon joined together in schools. As they explored the deep waters, months passed and seasons rolled into years. But even for big fish in large schools danger lurked.

Beneath the schools the warm-blooded porpoises hovered, invisible until they shot upwards, flipping at the last moment to snatch at the bellies of the salmon and cut them in two.

The dark shapes that darted to the surface to breath blocked the bright light of the sun as Swimmer dove, fear driving her toward the shadows. But in her flight she flashed her silver sides to an even greater enemy.

Pink   Chum   Coho   Sockeye   Chinook

The Orca was following the harbor porpoise when he smelled the salmon. Fifteen seasons past his birth, the Orca was nearly twenty feet long. In one motion he rolled after Swimmer.

Swimmer fled, pressing for the safety of a rocky ledge. The whale followed, slicing through sea, his white teeth ready to snap. Down, down, surging down, Swimmer could feel the whale's body behind her. Closer and closer, the huge jaws opened. The tug of the wake pulled toward the rows of deadly teeth. Then darkness.

Swimmer pressed her body against crusty rocks, breath ragged, blood pumping. The killer whale circled, it's nose bumping against her hiding place.

Then the Orca was gone, and, once again, Swimmer had survived.

Squid

Sandlance

Smelt

Herring

Crustaceans

The oceangoing Chinook is a robust fish, with a blue green tint on its back fading to silver on the sides and white on the belly. It has black gums. The Chinook feeds on herring, smelt, sandlance, squid and crustaceans. Salmon grow extremely fast in the ocean and can double their weight during a single summer.

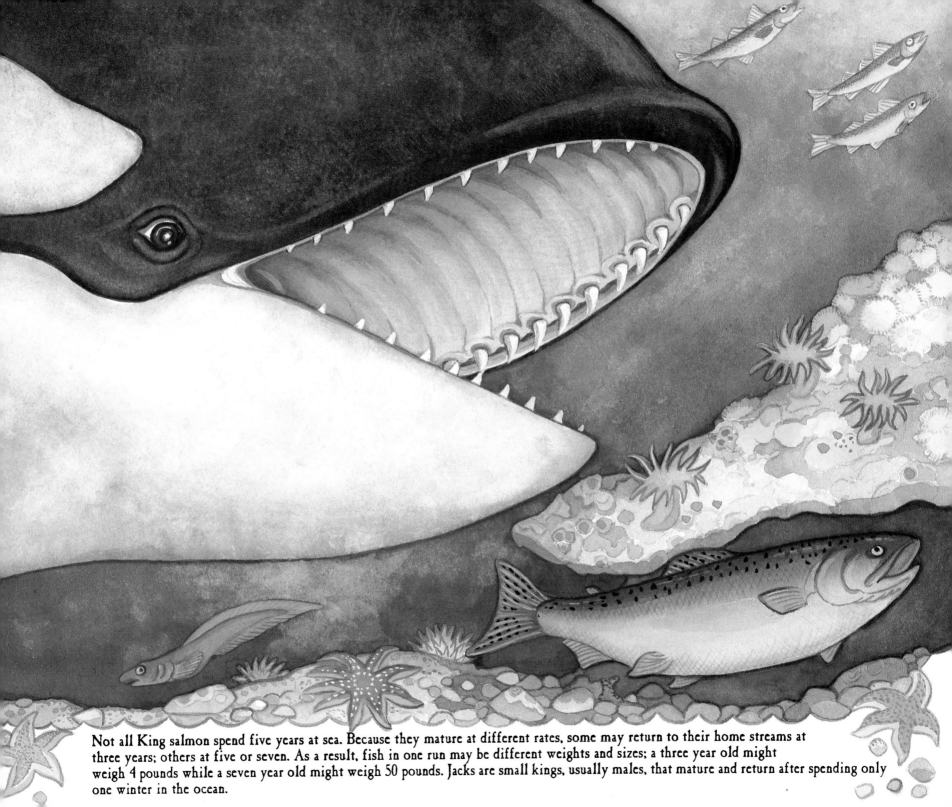

Not all King salmon spend five years at sea. Because they mature at different rates, some may return to their home streams at three years; others at five or seven. As a result, fish in one run may be different weights and sizes; a three year old might weigh 4 pounds while a seven year old might weigh 50 pounds. Jacks are small kings, usually males, that mature and return after spending only one winter in the ocean.

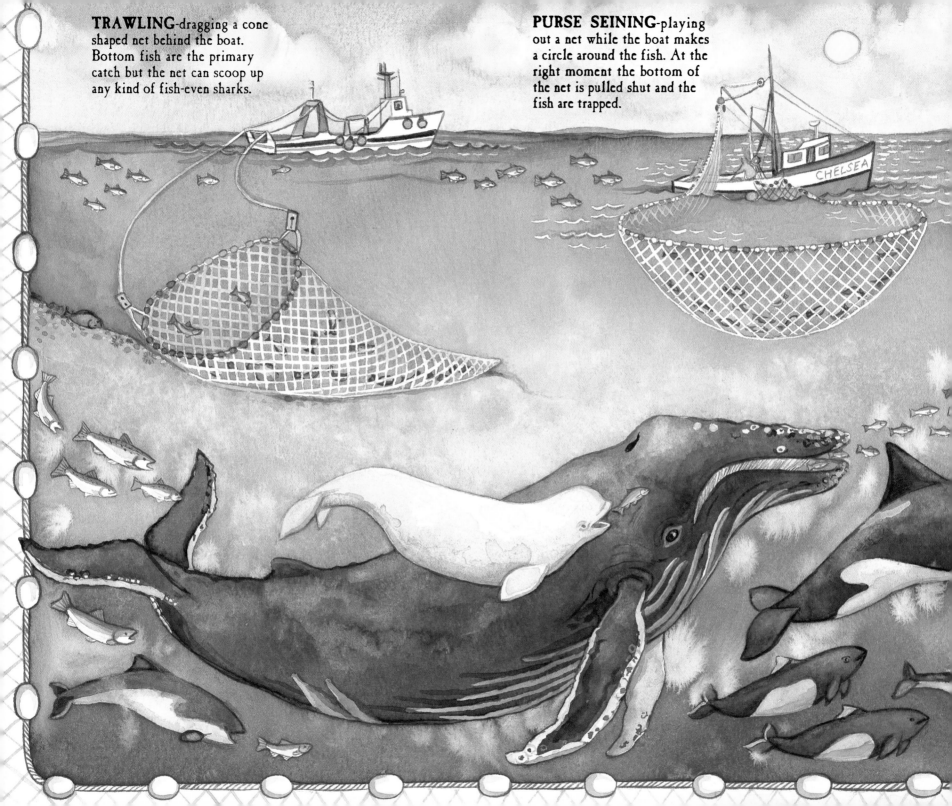

TRAWLING-dragging a cone shaped net behind the boat. Bottom fish are the primary catch but the net can scoop up any kind of fish-even sharks.

PURSE SEINING-playing out a net while the boat makes a circle around the fish. At the right moment the bottom of the net is pulled shut and the fish are trapped.

TROLLING-fishing with a pole and lure pulled at a steady speed behind an open boat.

GILLNETTING-fishing with long straight nets that can stretch up to 9 miles in length on the high seas. A certain size fish-salmon-are caught by the gills as they swim into the net. Some of these nets drift; some are anchored.

Swimmer followed mid-ocean currents in a counter-clockwise migration, up the coast of Alaska to the edge of the Bering Sea, then west into the deep waters of the Pacific. By the time she was five years old, Swimmer had traveled more than 10,000 miles, dodging whales and sharks and seals and the nets of the fishing fleets. Eat and avoid being eaten. That was Swimmer's life.

Then, in her fifth year, the ancient instincts that had driven her to leave the river of her birth and seek the sea told her it was time to go home.

She began her homeward migration in the spring. The geese were also winging north, honking in high flying formation as they headed to their nesting grounds.

Across the northern hemisphere animals shook off winter's spell and began to move. A caribou stopped to drink as she circled back to her Arctic calving grounds. Whales left the warm southern waters, joined by ringed seals, sea lions and walrus. All of them moved in their own rhythm. To find food, to mate, to survive.

Salmon from many rivers swim together in the same areas through much of their oceangoing life. As they approach maturity they leave the deep water for the coast and begin to seek out their parent stream. The salmon find their way back to their home river using currents, the earth's magnetic forces, and the stars. Once they get close to their home streams biologists think the fish smell their way back to the riffle in which they were born.

Scientists estimate there are over 1000 spawning populations of Chinooks on the North American coast. The largest rivers tend to have the largest runs and be the heaviest fished. The Yukon Kings are valued (and fished enthusiastically) because of the high oil content of their red flesh. Incidentally, some Southeast Alaskan salmon have white flesh.

As the salmon move into fresh water to spawn they stop eating, living off their accumulated fats. And they begin to change. They often take on a grisly appearance. The males develop hooked snouts and their skin begins to change color from healthy silver to splotchy red to light pink. Males are more deeply colored than females.

For Swimmer and the other salmon the journey back to the home creek was filled with danger. All along the Yukon fishermen stretched their nylon nets, hoping to catch salmon to eat and sell.

As Swimmer thrust past she could hear the pounding echo of the unlucky fish, their bodies banging against the hulls of the boats.

Further up river people fished with gill nets and dip nets, fish wheels and poles. Grizzly bears fished with mouth and claws while the wolverine and eagle fed on leftovers. Everyone depended on the returning fish to make them fat for winter.

Swimmer paid little attention to those who hunted her. She had only one purpose. To lay her eggs on a gravel bed near the birch where she was born.

Salmon are amazing not only in the distance they cover but in the speed they swim. Some Yukon Kings, bound for their spawning grounds in the Canadian Yukon Territory, will travel over 2000 river miles in a 60 day period. Kings are also high jumpers capable of leaping 10 feet in the air.

Familiar smells guided Swimmer to Caribou Creek. Beside her, behind her, swam more fish.

The deep water turned shallow and sometimes sharp rocks cut her, but Swimmer hardly noticed.

Down river at fish camp, women split their catch at the belly with sharp knives then stripped the salmon to hang on alder poles in the smokehouse. Katya, now 11 years old, paused from her chores at the river's edge. She flicked her storyknife across the mud with the same motion Swimmer used to flick her tale, digging her nest upstream in the gravel. A male salmon hovered nearby. As Swimmer dropped her precious eggs, he covered them with a cloud of milky sperm. With powerful sweeps of her tail Swimmer buried the nest, then she pushed up the river, her energy waning, her life slipping away. Soon the circle would close. She built another nest, and another and another. If one was destroyed another might survive.

Female digging nest

Dropping milt and eggs

Female burying eggs

The female salmon distributes between 2000-5000 eggs in several different nests. The nests or underwater nurseries are called redds. They are a circular depression made in the gravel of the river bottom. They may be fertilized with **milt** (sperm) by more than one male. Of the average 3000 eggs only about 300 survive as fry. Of those 300 only four or five will become adults. One or two of those will make it all the way back to their birthplace. These survivors may travel as much as 10,000 miles at sea as they dodge predators, people and pollution.

What kind of magic helped these mighty fish find their way back to Caribou Creek?

Katya wondered as she paused along the bank. But soon the girl was drawn up the trail by the smells of her camp, the fry bread, the drying fish, the wood smoke. She was at the beginning of her own journey and had much to learn. Like Swimmer, Katya would face danger and sadness, struggling against the current, at times feeling battered and bruised. Yet she would always remember the brave beauty of the salmon. Flinging their silver bodies in the sunlight. Flexing, jumping in the ancient fierce dance that brought them back to the place where the circle closed.

As Katya dreamed of adventures to come, Swimmer's adventure ended. Beneath the icy waters of Caribou Creek, the body that held her mighty spirit lay next to the roots of the old birch, crumbling bit by bit over the winter months, adding rich food to the water for the next generation of salmon to eat.

Near Swimmer's tail one bright orange egg tumbled along a sandy patch of bottom. Where the circled ended, the circle began.

Alaska's state fish goes by many names. Chinook, Spring, King and Blackmouth all describe the same fish. The Chinook is an anadromous fish: born in fresh water, she migrates to saltwater, matures, then returns to fresh water to spawn. Relatives of our modern Pacific Salmon evolved over 50 million years ago. 5-6 million years ago Sabertooth Salmon grew to ten feet in length, had fangs and weighed 500 lbs. The modern salmon has been around for 2 million years.

The salmon face great dangers from logging, dam construction, irrigation, destruction of wetlands, industrial pollution and fleets of commercial fishing vessels so high tech they are capable of catching every single salmon that would return to spawn. If the salmon are to survive, their way of life must be protected by the very creature who threatens them the most: man.

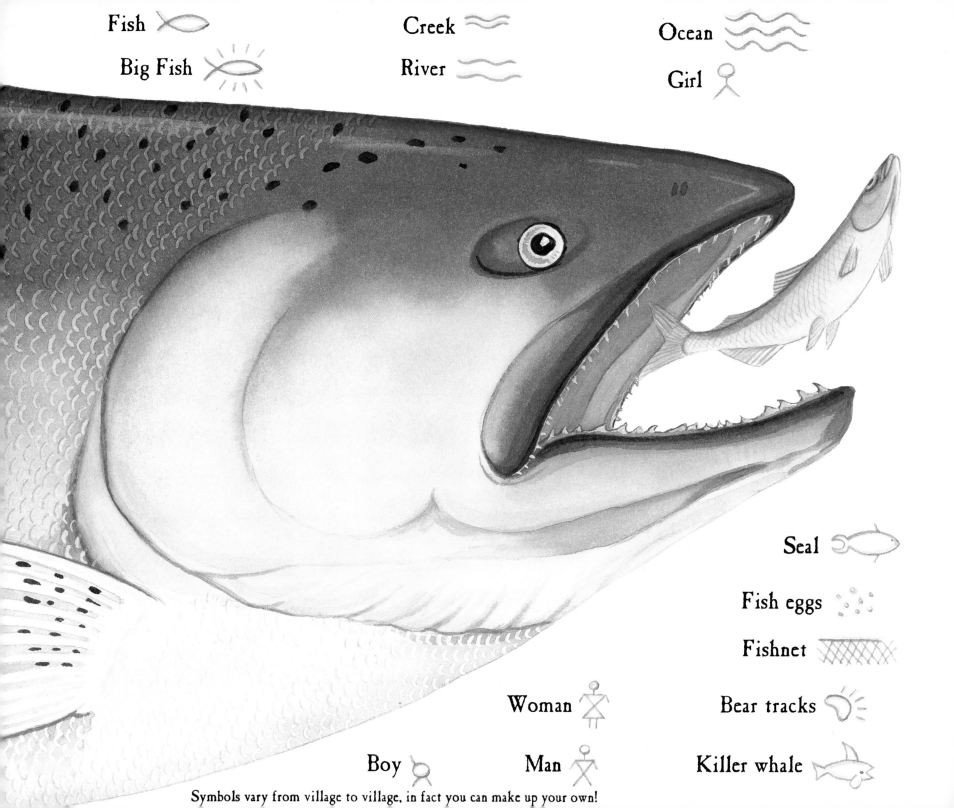

Fish

Big Fish

Creek

River

Ocean

Girl

Seal

Fish eggs

Fishnet

Bear tracks

Woman

Boy   Man   Killer whale

Symbols vary from village to village, in fact you can make up your own!